THE GNOCCHI
HORROR SHOW
COOKBOOK

THE GNOCCHI HORROR SHOW
COOKBOOK
50 BLOCKBUSTER MOVIE-INSPIRED RECIPES

BY LACHLAN HAYMAN

RECIPES DIRECTED BY
KARINA DUNCAN

DOG 'N' BONE

DEDICATED TO
RICE WITHASPOON

First published in 2017 as *The Lambshank Redemption Cookbook*.
This revised edition published in 2023 by Dog 'n' Bone Books
An imprint of Ryland Peters & Small Ltd

20–21 Jockey's Fields 341 E 116th St
London WC1R 4BW New York, NY 10029

www.rylandpeters.com

10 9 8 7 6 5 4 3 2 1

Text © Lachlan Hayman 2017, 2023
Design and photography © Dog 'n' Bone Books 2017, 2023

A CIP catalog record for this book is available from the Library
of Congress and the British Library.

ISBN: 978 1 912983 63 6

Printed in China

Editor: Caroline West
Designer: Wide Open Studio
Photographer: Stephen Conroy
Photography styling and art direction: Tonia Shuttleworth
Home economist: Ellie Jarvis
Additional photography credits: pages 6–7 by Kate Whitaker; pages
140–141 by WIlliam Lingwood; page 144 by Isobel Wield

MIX
Paper | Supporting
responsible forestry
FSC® C008047

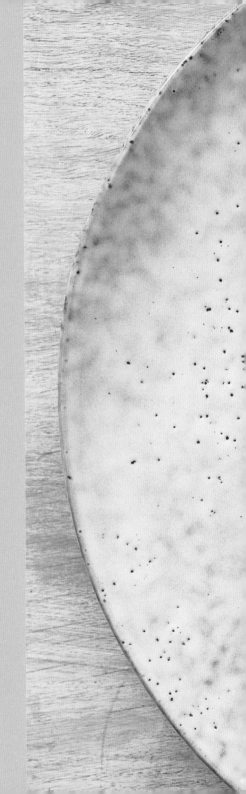

CONTENTS

LIGHTS, KORMA, ACTION!

INTRODUCTION

Armageddon hungry. And if you're like me, you'll enjoy sitting down in front of the screen for some blockbuster cuisine with a pinch of Sheen... and the odd glass of Legally Blanc.

Do you like your shanks with a side of Hanks? Your porcini with a sprinkle of Pacino? Then look no further.

Even the combined forces of Mutton Scorsese, Clint Feastwood, Ramen Polanski, David Lunch, Jams Cameron, and Medley Scott couldn't cast anything so moreish. Call it the Silver Linings Cookbook.

Enjoy!

MAY THE FORKS BE WITH YOU

HONEY, I DRUNK THE KIDS

MURDER IN THE THIRST

THE LAST OF THE MOJITOS

FORGETTING SYRAH MARSHALL

LEGALLY BLANC

LAWRENCE OF ARABICA

MATCHA POINT

WHISKEY BUSINESS

THE COLA EXPRESS

12 BEERS A SLAVE

CANNONBALL RUM

THE BRIDGE ON THE RIVER CHAI

HOW THE QUENCH STOLE CHRISTMAS

HARRY POT AND THE PHILOSOPHER'S STOVE

WOK OF AGES

MONSTER'S BOWL

ONE FLEW OVER THE COOKER'S NEST

BEATER PAN

THE FRIDGES OF MADISON COUNTY

THE GRATE GATSBY

THE USUAL SAUCEPANS

SPOONRISE KINGDOM

THE DARK KNIFE

THREE MEN AND A BARBIE

BLACK FORK DOWN

THE NUTTY PROCESSOR

CHAPTER 1

BEST

DRAMAS

DALLAS BUYERS CRAB

Linguine with Crab, Chili, and Garlic

The rodeo-side fodder of Dallas, Texas, may be a far cry from this extravagant dish, but lasting 10 seconds on a raging bull deserves a grand reward. Saddle up.

1lb 2oz (500g) linguine

3 garlic cloves, finely chopped

1 red chili pepper, finely chopped and deseeded if required

10½oz (300g) crabmeat, from the fishmonger

½ cup (120ml) extra virgin olive oil

Zest and juice of 1 lemon

½ cup (15g) finely chopped parsley leaves

Salt and freshly ground black pepper

– Place a large pan of salted water over a high heat and cook the linguine according to the packet instructions.

– While the linguine is cooking, place the garlic, chili pepper, crabmeat, olive oil, and lemon juice and zest in a large bowl. Use a fork to mix the ingredients together until well combined. Drain the linguine once cooked and return to the empty pan. Add the crab mixture and mix well, coating all the linguine.

– Add the parsley and season with salt and pepper. Toss well to combine and serve immediately.

SERVES	4–6
PREPARATION TIME	40 MINUTES
COOKING TIME	30 MINUTES

QUICHE ME IF YOU CAN

Potato, Caramelized Onion, and Rosemary Frittata

2 tablespoons olive oil

2 onions, thinly sliced

1 tablespoon brown sugar

1 tablespoon chopped rosemary leaves

8 eggs

¼ cup (50ml) milk

2 cups (200g) grated mozzarella

1 garlic clove, crushed

1lb 2oz (500g) potatoes (such as Desiree or Yukon Gold), peeled, boiled, and sliced

Salt and freshly ground black pepper

Catch Me If You Can is the autobiographical movie of a master of deception who successfully posed as a pilot, doctor, and attorney. This is the story of a frittata pretending to be a quiche.

- Preheat the oven to 350°F/180°C/Gas 4.

- Heat half the olive oil in a large, ovenproof skillet (frying pan) over a medium heat. Add the onions and stir gently for 5 minutes or until golden. Add the brown sugar and cook for a further 3–4 minutes, or until the onions have caramelized. Remove from the heat, stir through the rosemary, and leave to cool.

- Use a whisk to beat the eggs and milk together in a large bowl. Using a wooden spoon, stir in half the mozzarella and the garlic, and season with salt and pepper. Add the cooked potatoes and cooled onions and rosemary, and then gently toss to combine.

- Heat the remaining olive oil over a low heat in the skillet (frying pan). Pour the frittata mixture into the pan and arrange the potato evenly in layers over the base. Cook for 2–3 minutes, and then sprinkle over the remaining mozzarella.

- Transfer the frittata to the oven and cook for 15 minutes, or until set, puffed, and golden.

- Remove the frittata from the oven and transfer carefully to a plate. Serve warm.

SERVES	6
PREPARATION TIME	15 MINUTES
COOKING TIME	1 HOUR

LENTIL MISS SUNSHINE

Lentil and Roast Tomato Soup

7 plum or Roma
tomatoes, halved

4 tablespoons olive oil

2 teaspoons cumin
seeds

2 teaspoons coriander
seeds

1 onion, chopped

3 garlic cloves, chopped

½ teaspoon ground
turmeric

Pinch of saffron threads

½ red chili pepper, finely
chopped and deseeded
if required

¾ cup (150g) red lentils

3¾ cups (900ml) chicken
or vegetable stock

Salt and freshly ground
black pepper

½ cup (125g) Greek
yogurt, to serve

Apart from the fantastic character portrayals, the star of this superb flick is surely the vintage Volkswagen Type 2 camper van. It inspired my free-spirited boho soup. Its yellow color also prompted the use of turmeric.

– Preheat the oven to 350°F/180°C/Gas 4.

– Place the tomatoes (cut side up) on a baking tray lined with baking paper. Drizzle over half the olive oil and season with salt and pepper. Cook in the oven for 40 minutes.

– Meanwhile, toast the cumin and coriander seeds in a pan over a medium heat for 2 minutes or until aromatic. Remove from the heat and leave to cool for 5 minutes. Once cool, place in a mortar and pestle (or spice grinder) and grind together. Set aside.

– Once the tomatoes are ready, remove them from the oven. Set aside.

– Heat the remaining olive oil in a large saucepan over a medium heat. Add the onion and sauté for 5 minutes. Add the ground spices, garlic, turmeric, saffron, and chili pepper. Stir to combine and cook for 2 minutes. Add the lentils, roasted tomatoes, and stock. Stir through all the ingredients and bring to a simmer. Cook for 20 minutes, stirring from time to time.

– Once the soup is ready, season with salt and pepper and serve with a spoonful of yogurt swirled through.

SERVES	4
PREPARATION TIME	15 MINUTES
COOKING TIME	30 MINUTES

1lb 2oz (500g) baby carrots, trimmed and peeled (optional)

2 tablespoons olive oil

1 teaspoon cumin seeds

1 teaspoon ground sumac

½ cup (85g) quinoa, rinsed

3 avocados

3½ cups (100g) baby spinach

3 scallions (spring onions), sliced

3 tablespoons raisins

4 tablespoons pumpkin seeds, toasted

Salt and freshly ground black pepper

For the dressing:

Scant ½ cup (100ml) extra virgin olive oil

1 tablespoon red wine vinegar

Zest and juice of 1 orange

GRAIN MAN

Roast Carrot, Avocado, and Quinoa Salad

What foods are packed full of nutrients that help to promote brain health? Avocados, spinach, carrots, whole grains, and seeds. Well, looky here. It appears that this salad might give you the same memory and card-counting skills as Dustin Hoffman's award-winning character Raymond (aka "Rain Main").

– Preheat the oven to 350°F/180°C/Gas 4.

– Place the carrots in a large roasting pan and drizzle over the olive oil. Add the cumin seeds and sumac, and season with salt and pepper. Toss well to combine. Transfer the pan to the oven and roast the carrots for 30 minutes, or until they are tender.

– Meanwhile, cook the quinoa according to the packet instructions. Drain and leave to cool in a large bowl.

– To make the dressing, whisk all the ingredients together in a small bowl. Season with salt and pepper, and set aside.

– Once the quinoa is cool, add the cooked carrots, avocado, spinach, scallions (spring onions), raisins, and dressing to the mixing bowl. Toss to combine. Place the salad on a platter and scatter with the pumpkin seeds.

– Serve slightly warm or at room temperature.

SERVES	4
PREPARATION TIME	20 MINUTES
COOKING TIME	1 HOUR

BOOGIE NUTS

Roast Beet and Feta Salad with Macadamia Dukkah

6 medium beets
(beetroot), ends
trimmed

½ cup (70g) feta, roughly
crumbled

1 red onion, thinly sliced

*For the Macadamia
Dukkah:*

½ cup (60g) macadamia
nuts

2 tablespoons sesame
seeds

1 tablespoon coriander
seeds

1 tablespoon cumin
seeds

¼ teaspoon salt

For the dressing:

3 tablespoons extra
virgin olive oil

3 tablespoons red wine
vinegar

Inspired by a film about the golden age of
the porn industry, it's no coincidence that
this hardcore salad contains nuts and a root
vegetable. Just wait for the happy ending.

– Preheat the oven to 400°F/200°C/Gas 6.

– Wrap each of the beets (beetroot) in aluminum foil and place
on a baking tray. Bake for 1 hour or until the beets are tender
when pierced with a knife. Remove from the oven and set aside
to cool slightly. Once cool enough to handle, use your hands or a
knife to peel the beets. Cut each beet into medium-sized pieces
(about 1¼–2in/3–5cm).

– To make the dukkah, place the macadamia nuts, sesame seeds,
coriander seeds, cumin seeds, and salt in a medium skillet
(frying pan) over a medium heat. Fry the nuts and seeds for
3 minutes, stirring regularly. Remove from the heat and set
aside to cool completely. Once cool, place the mixture in
a food processor (or use a mortar and pestle) and process
until roughly ground.

– Place the beets, feta, onion, and dukkah in a large bowl.

– To make the dressing, whisk the olive oil and red wine vinegar
together in a small bowl.

– Drizzle the dressing over the beet salad and toss gently to
combine all the ingredients before serving.

SERVES	4
PREPARATION TIME	10 MINUTES
COOKING TIME	30 MINUTES

BRATWURST AT TIFFANY'S

Bangers and Mustard Mash with Caramelized Red Onion Gravy

2lb (900g) potatoes, peeled and chopped into medium cubes

¼ cup (50ml) milk

4 tablespoons (50g) butter

¼ cup (5g) chopped parsley leaves (optional)

2 tablespoons olive oil

8 gourmet pork sausages

1 red onion, thinly sliced

2 tablespoons traditional gravy powder

1 teaspoon Dijon mustard

1 cup (250ml) hot beef stock

Salt and freshly ground black pepper

Tiffany & Co is renowned for its fine silver; this time it's knives and forks. Show that special one you care by serving the sausages in an elegant aqua-blue box.

- Place the potatoes in a large saucepan and cover with cold water. Bring to a boil and cook for 12–15 minutes, or until the potatoes are tender. Drain the potatoes and allow to steam-dry. Add the milk and butter, and season with salt and pepper. Mash the potatoes until smooth and stir through the parsley, if using. Cover the pan with a lid and keep warm until ready to serve.

- While the potatoes are cooking, heat half the olive oil in a large, heavy-based skillet (frying pan) over a medium heat. Add the sausages and fry for 10 minutes, turning regularly to ensure they are completely cooked through. Once cooked, transfer the sausages to a plate and cover to keep warm.

- Heat the remaining olive oil in the same pan over a medium heat. Add the onion and cook for 10–12 minutes or until golden and caramelized. Add the gravy powder and mustard, and stir until combined. Gradually add the beef stock and mix well. Cook for 5 minutes or until the gravy begins to thicken.

- Serve the sausages alongside the mash and spoon over the gravy.

Ingredients

2 lamb backstrap or loin fillets (around 1lb 2oz/500g)

1 tablespoon olive oil

4 large pita wraps or Lebanese-style bread

For the tabbouleh:

½ cup (75g) bulgur wheat

1 tomato, deseeded and finely chopped

¼ cup (50ml) lemon juice

1 small cucumber, peeled and finely chopped

½ red onion, finely chopped

1 cup (25g) chopped parsley leaves

½ cup (15g) chopped mint leaves

For the hummus:

2 x 14oz (400g) cans chickpeas, drained

1 tablespoon tahini

2 garlic cloves, crushed

2 tablespoons lemon juice

⅓ cup (70ml) olive oil

Salt and freshly ground black pepper

THE HUMMUS CROWN AFFAIR

Lamb, Tabbouleh, and Hummus Wraps

SERVES	4
PREPARATION TIME	40 MINUTES
COOKING TIME	15 MINUTES

This recipe is a masterpiece worth stealing. The movie portrays a billionaire who successfully burgles The Metropolitan Museum of Art. So, it's only fitting that our dish contains "burghul" (or bulgur wheat). Now, see if you can remove all the seeds from the tomato without anyone noticing.

– To make the tabbouleh, place the bulgur wheat, tomato, and lemon juice in a small bowl. Set aside for 30 minutes or until the bulgur wheat is soft.

– To make the hummus, place the chickpeas, tahini, garlic, and lemon juice in a food processor. Blitz the ingredients and then slowly pour in the olive oil while the processor is running. Once the mixture is smooth, season with salt and pepper, and then quickly process again. Tip the mixture into a bowl and set aside.

– Brush the lamb with the olive oil and season with salt and pepper. Place the lamb in a large, non-stick skillet (frying pan) over a medium-high heat. Cook for 3 minutes on each side for medium (2–3 minutes longer for medium to well-done). Transfer the lamb to a plate, cover with aluminum foil, and leave to rest while you finish making the tabbouleh. Once rested, thinly slice the lamb.

– To finish the tabbouleh, place the cucumber, onion, parsley, and mint in a medium bowl. Add the soaked bulgur wheat and tomato, and toss to combine.

– To serve, spread a spoonful of hummus over the bread, add a quarter of the sliced lamb, and top with a generous amount of tabbouleh.

BEST ACTOR OF ALL TIME

And the nominees are...

AL PORCINI	CHRISTIAN KALE
ANTHONY NAPKINS	CHUTNEY SHEEN
BEAN AFFLECK	CRAY LIOTTA
BRAD SPIT	CRESS HEMSWORTH
BRAMLEY COOPER	CURD RUSSELL
BREAD ASTAIRE	DANNY DORITO
CARVIN' COSTNER	DANNY GUAVA
CHEEK GYLLENHAAL	EATIN' HAWKE
CHEF GOLDBLUM	ERROL FLAN
CHIVE OWEN	FILLET SEYMOUR HOFFMAN
CHOOK NORRIS	GOOSE WILLIS
CHRIS RACK	HARRISON FOOD

HUMPHREY NOUGAT	MUSSEL CROWE
JAMIE FORKS	PANTRY SWAYZE
JEFF FRIDGES	RADICCHIO DEL TORO
JOHNNY DIP	REUBEN WILLIAMS
JONAH DILL	ROBERT DEVOUR
JUDE SLAW	ROBERT DOWNEY TUNA
KAFFIR SUTHERLAND	RYAN GOZLEME
KEVIN SPICEY	SAMUEL EEL JACKSON
LAMB NEESON	SHIA LEBEEF
LAURENCE FISHBONE	STEVE SASHIMI
LIVER PHOENIX	STEWIN' MCGREGOR
MACKEREL J FOX	TOM SHANKS
MEAT DAMON	TOMMY LEEK JONES
MICHAEL CAYENNE	WILLIAM H PASTRY
MINCE VAUGHAN	ZAC SAFFRON

SERVES	4
PREPARATION TIME	30 MINUTES
COOKING TIME	1 HOUR

GOOD DILL HUNTING

Flaky Salmon and Dill Pie

Here's both a flick and a dish to warm the cockles. This feel-good drama was written by virtual unknowns Matt Damon and Ben Affleck for one of Damon's Harvard screenplay assignments. The character of Will Hunting is an unrecognized genius with a knack for mathematics. They say just one serving of fish per week can increase your gray matter and IQ. Here goes.

2 tablespoons olive oil

2 tablespoons (25g) butter, plus 6 tablespoons (80g), melted

4 leeks (white part only), thinly sliced

3 garlic cloves, finely chopped

1¾lb (800g) fresh salmon, skin removed and cut into chunks

3 tablespoons chopped dill

8 sheets phyllo (filo) pastry

Salt and freshly ground black pepper

Green salad or green beans, to serve

- Preheat the oven to 400°F/200°C/Gas 6.

- Heat the olive oil and the 2 tablespoons (25g) of butter in a large, 10–11in (25–28cm), non-stick ovenproof skillet (frying pan) over a medium heat. Once the butter has melted, add the leek and garlic, and cook for 8–10 minutes or until softened. Transfer the ingredients to a large bowl, add the salmon and dill, and season with salt and pepper. Toss to combine all the ingredients.

- Clean the skillet (frying pan), and then lightly grease with a small amount of the melted butter. Place one sheet of phyllo (filo) pastry on a clean surface and use a pastry brush to brush with some of the melted butter. Place the sheet of phyllo in the pan (leaving the edges overhanging). Brush another sheet of phyllo with more melted butter and place at an angle on top of the first sheet to start covering the base of the pan. Repeat this process, overlapping the sheets of phyllo as you go, until all the sheets are used.

- Spoon the salmon filling into the pastry case and fold over the sheets of overhanging phyllo—add another sheet or two if they don't quite cover the top of the pie. Transfer to the oven and bake for 20 minutes. Carefully turn the pan over onto a baking tray, so that the base of the pie becomes the top. Bake for a further 20 minutes or until golden.

- Serve immediately with a green salad or some green beans.

THE LAMBSHANK REDEMPTION

Braised Lamb Shanks with Cheesy Polenta

3 tablespoons all-purpose (plain) flour

8 lamb shanks, trimmed

2 tablespoons olive oil

8 shallots, peeled and halved

1 cup (250ml) red wine

3 cups (700ml) beef stock

14oz (400g) can chopped tomatoes

1 tablespoon balsamic vinegar

2 tablespoons chopped rosemary leaves

3 tablespoons chopped parsley leaves, to serve

For the Cheesy Polenta:

4 cups (1 liter) water

2 cups (500ml) chicken stock

2 cups (375g) cornmeal (polenta)

⅓ cup (80ml) heavy (double) cream

¾ cup (70g) freshly grated Parmesan cheese

Salt and freshly ground black pepper

SERVES	4
PREPARATION TIME	15 MINUTES
COOKING TIME	1¼ HOURS

If these shanks were served as jail food, everyone would commit felonies or climb up tied bedsheets just to get in. And, as they say: "If you do the crime, you've gotta do the time." Hence why you slow-braise these babies for an hour. Anyway, what's the rush if you're doing life?

- Place the flour in a large bowl. Add the lamb shanks and toss to dust on all sides. Shake off any excess flour.

- Heat half the olive oil in a large, deep-sided skillet (frying pan) over a medium heat. Once the oil is hot, fry the lamb shanks on all sides until browned. Remove from the pan and set aside.

- Heat the remaining oil in the pan and fry the shallots for 5 minutes or until golden. Return the lamb to the pan and add the wine, beef stock, tomatoes, vinegar, and rosemary. Gently stir to combine and then bring to a boil. Once boiling, reduce the heat to low and cover the pan with a lid. Cook for 1 hour.

- To make the polenta, bring the water and chicken stock to a boil in a large saucepan over a high heat. Once boiling, gradually add the cornmeal (polenta) in a steady stream, stirring constantly with a wooden spoon. Reduce the heat to low and continue to stir for 2 minutes or until the cornmeal becomes soft. Remove from the heat, then add the cream and Parmesan cheese. Season with salt and pepper, and stir well to combine. Set aside until the shanks are ready.

- Remove the shanks from the pan and transfer to a large bowl. Increase the heat to high and simmer the sauce uncovered for 10 minutes, or until reduced and thickened. Return the shanks to the pan and season with salt and pepper.

- Serve the Cheesy Polenta topped with the lamb shanks and sauce. Finish with a sprinkle of parsley.

CHILI CHILI BANG BANG

SEX, LIES & VINDALOO TAPE

SATAY NIGHT FEVER

THE MADRAS OF KING GEORGE

CROUCHING TIKKA, HIDDEN DRAGON

DIRTY ROTI SCOUNDRELS

NAANS ON THE RUN

DAHL M FOR MURDER

THE NEVER RENDANG STORY

FLASH GARDEN

RADICCHIO & JULIET

YOU'VE GOT KALE

FULL NETTLE JACKET

CABBAGE UNDER FIRE

REBEL WITHOUT A COS

THE PEA SHOOT OF HAPPINESS

INTERVIEW WITH THE SAMPHIRE

SINGLE WHITE FENNEL

SERVES	2
PREPARATION TIME	15 MINUTES
COOKING TIME	30 MINUTES, PLUS RESTING

GOOD MORNAY, VIETNAM

Broiled Lobster Mornay

1 medium cooked lobster, halved and cleaned

1¼ cups (300ml) milk

1 onion, sliced

1 bay leaf

6 black peppercorns

2 tablespoons (30g) butter

2 tablespoons all-purpose (plain) flour

Pinch of nutmeg

2 tablespoons light (single) cream

¼ cup (5g) chopped parsley leaves

¼ cup (5g) snipped chives

¼ cup (25g) grated Cheddar cheese

¼ cup (25g) grated Gruyère cheese

Salt and freshly ground black pepper

Mixed salad leaves, to serve

Attention army bisque jockeys: if you want to rally the troops, cast this lobster delicacy out across the airwaves. It puts the station in crustacean.

– Remove the meat from the tail, legs, and body of the lobster. Cut the lobster meat into ¾in (2cm) pieces, place in a bowl, and refrigerate. Wash and dry the lobster shells, and reserve for later.

– In a medium saucepan, bring the milk, onion, bay leaf, and peppercorns to a simmer. Remove from the heat and leave to stand for 15 minutes to infuse the flavors. Strain the milk through a fine sieve and discard the onion, bay leaf, and peppercorns.

– In a separate medium saucepan, melt the butter over a medium heat. Add the flour and stir for 1–2 minutes. Gradually add the infused milk while stirring with a whisk. Continue to whisk until the mixture reaches a simmer and becomes smooth and thick. Add the nutmeg, season with salt and pepper, and stir through the cream. Remove from the heat, and stir through the lobster pieces, parsley, and chives.

– Divide the lobster mixture between the two half shells and sprinkle over the cheeses. Place under the broiler (grill) for 2–3 minutes, or until the cheeses melt and turn golden.

– Serve the lobster with a side salad of mixed leaves (optional).

THE KING'S PEACH

Peach and Mint Sorbet

12 large, ripe peaches

1½ cups (300g) sugar

1½ cups (375ml) water

2 teaspoons lemon juice

6 mint leaves, chopped

Pinch of salt

Dry mouth? Stuttering your words? Before you address the peasants, recruit the services of a peach therapist and soothe the vocal chords with this refreshing and cool sorbet. It speaks volumes.

– Peel the peaches and slice them into 1¼in (3cm) pieces. Place in a container and freeze for 2 hours or until completely firm.

– Place the sugar and water in a food blender and mix to combine. Add the frozen peaches, lemon juice, mint, and salt. Blend until the mixture becomes smooth and creamy.

– Serve immediately or place in a container and freeze for up to 3 days.

SERVES	8
PREPARATION TIME	15 MINUTES, PLUS COOLING TIME (PREPARE 24 HOURS IN ADVANCE)
COOKING TIME	1 HOUR 10 MINUTES

9 extra-large (large) eggs

1¾ cups (350g) superfine (caster) sugar

1¼ cups (300ml) heavy (double) cream

1½ cups (350ml) passionfruit juice, strained, plus extra seeds for garnish (optional)

1 large sheet of frozen sweet pie crust (shortcrust pastry), thawed

1 beaten egg, for the egg wash

THE PASSION OF THE CRUST

Heavenly Passionfruit Tart

Hallelujah! A dessert worthy of The Last Supper to satisfy a sweet tooth of biblical proportions. It's so moreish, you'll leave nun behind…

- Whisk the eggs in a large bowl. Add the sugar and continue whisking until the sugar and eggs are combined. While gently stirring, pour in the cream and passionfruit juice, and continue to stir until everything is well blended. Cover with plastic wrap (clingfilm) and refrigerate overnight.

- Preheat the oven to 350°F/180°C/Gas 4. Carefully line a 10in (26cm) tart pan (tin) with a sheet of pie crust (shortcrust pastry), pushing in the sides gently so it sits snugly in the pan. Rest in the refrigerator for 30 minutes.

- Remove any overhanging pie crust (pastry) and then line the tart case with aluminum foil. Place some rice on the foil and bake blind in the oven for 20 minutes. Remove the rice and foil, and brush the case with the egg wash. Bake in the oven for a further 10 minutes.

- Remove the tart case from the oven and lower the temperature to 275°F/130°C/Gas 1. Once the oven reaches temperature, return the case to the oven. With the case sitting in the oven, carefully pour in the passionfruit custard. Fill the tart right to the top. Bake for 40 minutes or until slightly wobbly in the middle.

- Remove the tart from the oven and leave to cool for 1 hour before removing from the tart pan. Serve at room temperature, sprinkling over some fresh passionfruit seeds as a garnish (optional).

SERVES   10
PREPARATION TIME   20 MINUTES
COOKING TIME   1½ HOURS PLUS COOLING

CHERRY MAGUIRE

French Meringues with Cherry Compote

Show them the money with these deal-clinchers
inspired by Cuba Pudding Jnr.

4 egg whites

Pinch of salt

1 cup (220g) superfine
(caster) sugar

½ teaspoon vanilla
extract

Whipped cream, to serve

For the Cherry Compote:

4 cups (700g) cherries,
pitted and halved

1 cup (250ml) red wine

2 tablespoons sugar

1 tablespoon orange
zest

– Preheat the oven to 250°F/120°C/Gas ½. Line two baking trays with baking paper.

– Whisk the egg whites and salt in the bowl of an electric mixer until they form soft peaks. Gradually add the sugar, one tablespoon at a time, whisking after each addition until the sugar has dissolved. Add the vanilla extract and whisk for a further 3 minutes on high speed until the mixture is thick and glossy.

– Place tablespoon-sized blobs of the meringue mixture on the prepared trays. Leave a 3–4in (8–10cm) gap between each meringue, as they will expand when baked.

– Reduce the oven temperature to 195°F/90°C/Gas ¼ and place the trays in the oven. Bake the meringues for 1½ hours and turn off the oven. Leave the meringues in the oven to cool completely.

– Meanwhile, to make the cherry compote, heat the cherries, wine, sugar, and orange zest in a medium saucepan over a medium heat. Bring to a simmer and cook for 10 minutes, stirring regularly. Remove the compote from the heat and leave to cool.

– Serve the meringues alongside the cherry compote and with a dollop of whipped cream.

CHAPTER 2 BEST COMEDY FILMS

SERVES	12
PREPARATION TIME	5 MINUTES

OYSTER POWERS: THE SPY WHO SHUCKED ME

Freshly Shucked Oysters with Champagne Vinaigrette

They say oysters are an aphrodisiac. So, if you've lost your mojo, just down a few of these saucy delights and go "undercovers." Groovy baby.

2 tablespoons Champagne vinegar

1 tablespoon Champagne (optional)

1 shallot, very finely chopped

1 tablespoon finely chopped tarragon leaves

12 oysters, freshly shucked

Salt and freshly ground black pepper

– In a small bowl, mix together the Champagne vinegar, Champagne (if using), shallot, and tarragon. Season with salt and black pepper.

– Arrange the oysters on a bed of crushed ice and serve with a teaspoon of the Champagne vinaigrette on each oyster. Serve immediately.

SERVES	4
PREPARATION TIME	15 MINUTES
COOKING TIME	10 MINUTES

SCHOOL OF WOK

Fried Rice with Jumbo Shrimp

4 eggs

¼ cup (50ml) vegetable oil

1 onion, finely chopped

2 garlic cloves, finely chopped

4 dried Chinese sausages, sliced

1¼lb (600g) raw jumbo shrimp (king prawns), peeled, shelled, and deveined

1 cup (150g) frozen peas

5 cups (800g) cold cooked long-grain rice

¼ cup (50ml) fish sauce

3 tablespoons soy sauce

½ cup (15g) chopped cilantro (coriander) leaves

3 scallions (spring onions), sliced diagonally

2 tablespoons chopped chives

Freshly ground black pepper

Tip: Choose a wok made of heavy metal.

– Crack the eggs into a medium bowl and whisk to combine.

– Heat one tablespoon of the oil in a large wok or deep-sided saucepan over a high heat. Once hot, add the eggs and swirl them around the base to make an omelet of even thickness. Allow the omelet to cook for about 2 minutes before carefully flipping it over and cooking for a further 30 seconds on the other side.

– Carefully transfer the omelet to a plate or board. Roll up the omelet and cut into thin slices.

– Heat the remaining oil in the wok or saucepan. Add the onion and garlic, and fry for 4–5 minutes until softened. Add the Chinese sausage, jumbo shrimp (king prawns), and peas, and cook for 2–3 minutes until the shrimp are cooked through. Add the rice, fish sauce, and soy sauce. Mix well to combine and cook for 2 minutes, stirring regularly to heat the rice. Stir through the sliced omelet.

– Remove from the heat, and add the cilantro (coriander), scallions (spring onions), and chives. Season with black pepper and mix well. Serve immediately.

SERVES	4
PREPARATION TIME	20 MINUTES
COOKING TIME	10 MINUTES

2 cups (100g) fresh breadcrumbs

2 tablespoons chopped dill leaves

4 firm white fish fillets (such as cod, halibut, or barramundi), boneless and skinless

½ cup (50g) all-purpose (plain) flour, for dusting

1 beaten egg

Vegetable oil, for frying

Salt and freshly ground black pepper

For the Fennel, Blood Orange, and Olive Salad:

2 baby fennel, trimmed and thinly sliced, with the tops reserved

2 blood oranges (or ordinary oranges), peeled and segmented, with pips and pith removed

½ cup (90g) Kalamata olives, pitted and halved

Zest and juice of 1 lemon (reserve the zest for the fish crumb)

2 tablespoons extra virgin olive oil

FRYING NEMO

Crumbed Fish with Fennel, Blood Orange, and Olive Salad

This dish serves as an adaptation of *Finding Nemo*—with a not-so-happy ending for the lead character, but a much more satisfying finale for the diner. I tried using kelp and sea cucumber for the salad, but it was a smidgen salty.

- To make the salad, place the fennel, oranges, and olives in a large mixing bowl. Add the lemon juice and extra virgin olive oil, and season with pepper. Toss very well to combine. Set aside to marinate while you prepare the fish.

- In a small bowl, mix together the breadcrumbs, dill, and one tablespoon of lemon zest. Set aside.

- Season the fish fillets with salt and pepper. Toss each fillet in the flour and shake off any excess. Dip the fillets in the beaten egg and then in the breadcrumbs until completely covered.

- Pour some vegetable oil into a deep-sided skillet (frying pan) until it sits ¾in (2cm) high up the sides of the pan. Place the pan over a medium heat. Once the oil is hot, shallow fry the fish fillets for 4–5 minutes on each side, or until they become crisp and golden. Remove the fish from the pan and soak up any excess oil on a plate lined with paper towel.

- Serve the fish alongside the salad, sprinkling over some of the reserved fennel tops for garnish.

DUDE, WHERE'S MY CAVIAR?

Taramasalata

Here's a dip inspired by dipsticks. Usually a delicacy reserved for the elite, this caviar spread is associated with two dopey pot-smokers who wake up unable to recall their reckless antics of the previous night. Let's hope they find their car and get back on the roe...

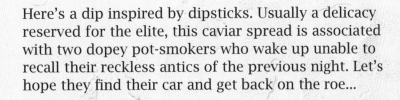

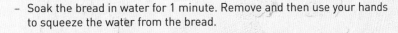

3½oz (100g) crustless white bread, torn into small pieces

3½oz (100g) salmon roe, plus extra to serve

1 shallot, finely chopped

½ garlic clove, finely chopped

1 cup (250ml) grapeseed oil

About 3 tablespoons (40ml) lemon juice

Salt and freshly ground black pepper

Crusty bread, toasted, to serve

- Soak the bread in water for 1 minute. Remove and then use your hands to squeeze the water from the bread.

- Add the bread to a food processor along with the salmon roe, shallot, and garlic. Process until smooth. With the motor running, gradually add the oil until the dip becomes thick and emulsified. Add the lemon juice and 3 tablespoons (40ml) of warm water, and season with salt and pepper. Mix to combine.

- Spoon the dip into a serving bowl, top with some extra roe, and serve with the toasted crusty bread.

PINE NUTS OF THE CARIBBEAN

Zucchini Carpaccio with Parmesan, Pine Nuts, and a Balsamic Dressing

Here's a dish worth walking the plank for. It's full of goodness to stave off the threat of scurvy. Just thinking about it is Jamaican me hungry.

1 zucchini (courgette)

¼ cup (25g) grated Parmesan cheese

2 tablespoons pine nuts, toasted

Salt and freshly ground black pepper

For the Balsamic Dressing:

1 tablespoon extra virgin olive oil

1 tablespoon balsamic vinegar

– Trim off the ends of the zucchini (courgette), and then use a knife or mandolin (or a sword) to slice the zucchini lengthwise as thinly as you can. Lay the slices in a single layer on a platter.

– To make the dressing, whisk the olive oil and balsamic vinegar together in a small bowl.

– Drizzle the dressing over the slices of zucchini. Season with salt and pepper, and then generously scatter over the Parmesan cheese and pine nuts.

– Serve alone as a starter or as a side to grilled fish or chicken.

2 small cucumbers, chopped into half moons

7oz (200g) cherry or mini Roma tomatoes, halved

1 red onion, thinly sliced

½ cup (90g) Kalamata olives, pitted and halved

Generous tablespoon (20ml) olive oil

10½oz (300g) halloumi, cut into ½in (1cm) slices

Juice of 1 lemon

3 mint sprigs, leaves only

Salt and freshly ground black pepper

For the dressing:

¼ cup (50ml) olive oil

¼ cup (50ml) lemon juice

¼ teaspoon dried oregano

MY BIG FAT GREEK SALAD

Greek Salad with Halloumi

If you're about to tie the knot, swap that dress for dressing because salad is the new cake. This one is a marriage of classic Greek ingredients. And, when you're done, celebrate by smashing the plate.

- Place the cucumber, tomatoes, onion, and olives in a large bowl.

- In another small bowl, mix the dressing ingredients together until combined. Pour the dressing over the salad and toss well to coat all the ingredients. Set aside.

- Heat the olive oil in a large skillet (frying pan) over a high heat for 1 minute. Add the halloumi slices and cook on each side for 2 minutes or until golden brown. Transfer the halloumi to a plate and then squeeze over the lemon juice. Add the halloumi and mint to the salad and season with salt and pepper.

- Gently toss all the ingredients together and serve immediately.

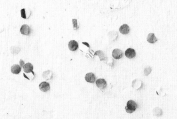

SERVES	4–5
PREPARATION TIME	10 MINUTES
COOKING TIME	5 HOURS

CUMIN TO AMERICA

Lemon, Mint, and Cumin Slow-Roast Lamb Shoulder

In *Coming to America*, Prince Akeem of Zamunda flees to the United States and goes undercover in a fast-food restaurant. At five hours' cooking time, our lamb shoulder is anything but fast. But it's well worth the wait. In fact, it'll make your soul glo.

1 tablespoon cumin seeds

3 tablespoons olive oil

3 garlic cloves, crushed

1 teaspoon dried mint

1 shoulder of lamb, bone in

Juice of 2 lemons

¼ cup (5g) roughly chopped mint leaves

Salt and freshly ground black pepper

– Preheat the oven to 300°F/150°C/Gas 2.

– Place the cumin seeds in a small skillet (frying pan) over a medium-high heat. Stir regularly for 3–4 minutes, or until the cumin seeds become aromatic and start to make "popping" noises. Transfer the seeds to a mortar and pestle, and grind to a coarse powder.

– Spread the ground cumin, olive oil, garlic, and dried mint over the lamb, and then season generously with salt and pepper. Place the lamb in a deep-sided roasting pan and squeeze over the juice of one of the lemons. Add water to the tray until it is ¾–1¼in (2–3cm) deep. Cover the tray with aluminum foil.

– Carefully transfer the lamb to the oven. Cook the lamb for 3 hours before removing the foil, then cook for a further 2 hours uncovered, basting with the juices every 30 minutes. Once cooked, remove the lamb from the oven and leave to rest for 10 minutes.

– Transfer the lamb to a serving platter, squeeze over the juice of the other lemon, and sprinkle with the chopped mint. Serve immediately.

Tip: Perhaps follow up with some Sexual Chocolate cocktails for dessert?

WEEKEND AT BÉARNAISE

Chargrilled Rib-Eye Steak with Tarragon Béarnaise

SERVES	4
PREPARATION TIME	15 MINUTES, PLUS MARINATING TIME
COOKING TIME	30 MINUTES

4 x 12oz (350g) rib-eye steaks, on the bone

⅓ cup (100ml) olive oil

2 garlic cloves, finely chopped

8 black peppercorns

4 tablespoons white wine vinegar

4 tablespoons white wine

2 shallots, finely chopped

3 tablespoons finely chopped tarragon leaves

3 egg yolks, at room temperature

1 tablespoon (15g) butter, cubed at room temperature

Salt and freshly ground black pepper

If your guests look as if they're about to go stiff, keep things alive with this delectable main. Fill a spare seat at the table by propping up a mannequin and get started.

- In a large bowl, marinate the steaks in the olive oil and garlic at room temperature for 30 minutes.

- Grind the peppercorns using a mortar and pestle until coarsely crushed.

- Place the peppercorns, vinegar, wine, shallots, and tarragon in a small saucepan over a high heat. Bring to a boil, and boil for 5 minutes or until the mixture reduces by half (there should be about 3 tablespoons/40ml remaining). Strain the liquid through a fine sieve into a pitcher (jug) and set aside.

- Set a broiler (grill) or barbecue to a high heat. Remove the steaks from the marinade and drain off any excess oil and garlic. Season the steaks generously with salt and pepper, and place under the broiler or on the barbecue. Cook for 4–5 minutes on each side (depending on the thickness) for medium-rare. Place the steaks on a warm plate and leave to rest for 8 minutes.

- Meanwhile, fill a saucepan a third- to a half-full with water. Put a heatproof mixing bowl on top of the pan, so that it fits snugly but is not touching the water below. Remove the bowl and bring the water to a simmer.

- Put the egg yolks and reserved liquid in the heatproof bowl, and place over the simmering water. Whisk the mixture until combined and reduce the heat to low. Continue whisking for 5–7 minutes or until a ribbon forms and the mixture holds its shape. Be careful not to let the mixture get too hot or it will curdle. Add the butter to the sauce one cube at a time, and whisk after each addition until the butter is incorporated into the sauce. Remove the bowl from the heat and season with salt and pepper. Carefully pour the sauce into a pitcher (jug).

- Slice the steaks and serve with the Béarnaise sauce.

SERVES	4
PREPARATION TIME	15 MINUTES
COOKING TIME	45 MINUTES

2 tablespoons vegetable oil

1 onion, finely sliced

3 garlic cloves, finely chopped

1¼in (3cm) piece of ginger, peeled and grated

2 teaspoons cumin seeds

1 tablespoon mild curry powder

1¼ cups (250g) dried red lentils, rinsed and drained

4 cups (1 liter) vegetable or chicken stock

¾ cup (200ml) coconut cream

10½oz (300g) sweet potato, peeled and diced into 1½–2in (4–5cm) pieces

Salt and freshly ground black pepper

Cooked jasmine or brown rice, to serve

For the Mint Yogurt:

½ cup (125g) natural yogurt

1 tablespoon finely chopped mint leaves

1 teaspoon lime juice

COOK-A-DAHL DUNDEE

Red Lentil and Sweet Potato Dahl with Mint Yogurt

Listen up Dahl. The link between Indian curries and Aussie bush tucker is a little tenuous, I know, but you could perhaps cook it in a croc pot... get it?

– Put the yogurt, mint, and lime juice in a small bowl. Season with salt and pepper, and mix all the ingredients together to combine. Set aside.

– Heat the oil in a large, deep-sided skillet (frying pan) or cooking pot over a medium heat. Add the onion and cook for 5 minutes or until softened. Add the garlic, ginger, cumin, and curry powder, and continue cooking for 4 minutes or until fragrant. Add the lentils, stock, and coconut cream, and bring to a simmer. Use a large spoon to remove any scum that rises to the surface.

– When the lentils reach a simmer, reduce the heat to low and cover the pan or pot. Continue to cook for 25 minutes, stirring occasionally. Add the sweet potato and cook for a further 10 minutes or until the potato is just tender. Season with salt and pepper. If the curry becomes too thick during cooking, add some extra water.

– Serve the curry with some rice and a spoonful of the minty yogurt accompaniment.

ASIAN'S ELEVEN

TOFU PANDA

ADMIT ONE · ADMIT ONE

DESPERATELY PEKING SUSAN

ADMIT ONE · ADMIT ONE

DESPICABLE MISO

ADMIT ONE · ADMIT ONE

GORENG THE DISTANCE

SOY STORY

ADMIT ONE · ADMIT ONE

STAND BAHN MI

ADMIT ONE · ADMIT ONE

ETERNAL SICHUAN OF A SPOTLESS MIND

ADMIT ONE · ADMIT ONE

MIAMI RICE

ADMIT ONE · ADMIT ONE

CHARIOTS OF PHO

ADMIT ONE · ADMIT ONE

PRETTY RAMEN

ADMIT ONE · ADMIT ONE

BENTO LIKE BECKHAM

THE SAUCE WHISPERER

AIOLI BABA &
THE FORTY
THIEVES

ADMIT ONE · ADMIT ONE

MUSTARD &
COMMANDER

ADMIT ONE · ADMIT ONE

THE GODS
MUST BE GRAVY

ADMIT ONE · ADMIT ONE

KETCHUP
IN THE RYE

ADMIT ONE · ADMIT ONE

NEAPOLITAN
DYNAMITE

10 THINGS
I HATE
ABOUT JUS

ADMIT ONE · ADMIT ONE

CHUTNEY'S
ANGELS

THE CURIOUS
CASE OF
BÉCHAMEL
BUTTON

ADMIT ONE · ADMIT ONE

ADMIT ONE

THE TEN
CONDIMENTS

ADMIT ONE

SERVES	4
PREPARATION TIME	15 MINUTES
COOKING TIME	12 MINUTES

4 skinless chicken thigh fillets, trimmed of fat

2 tablespoons olive oil

Zest and juice of 1 lemon

1 garlic clove, crushed

4 slices bacon

4 tablespoons aïoli

4 small ciabatta rolls or Turkish bread rolls, split

4 cups (50g) mixed salad leaves

1 avocado, peeled, halved, and sliced

Salt and freshly ground black pepper

WEDDING RASHERS

Chicken, Bacon, and Avocado Burgers

Any wedding that serves these burgers is definitely worth crashing. And what better meal to symbolize holy matrimony than one involving thighs and tasty buns. "Now for the exchange of the onion rings."

– Place one chicken thigh fillet in a large, plastic zip-lock bag, and use a meat mallet to pound the fillet until it is approximately ½in (1cm) thick. Repeat with the remaining fillets. Transfer the flattened fillets to a large bowl and add the olive oil, lemon zest and juice, and garlic. Season with salt and pepper, and toss well to coat the chicken.

– Cook the chicken on a barbecue (or in a grill pan over a high heat) for 3–4 minutes on each side or until cooked through. Once cooked, place the chicken on a plate and cover with aluminum foil to rest. Cook the bacon on the same barbecue (or grill pan) for 2 minutes on each side or until browned.

– Spread some aïoli over the base of each bread roll. Top with some salad leaves and sliced avocado, and then add the chicken and bacon. Close the burgers with the tops of the rolls and serve immediately.

TO COOK A MOCKINGBIRD

ZERO DUCK THIRTY

THIGH FIDELITY

GOOSE BUSTERS

THE FOUL MONTY

THE BREAST EXOTIC MARIGOLD HOTEL

THE NOTE CHOOK

QUAIL RIDER

LORD OF THE WINGS

FEATHER OF THE BRIDE

DANTE'S BEAK

CLEAR AND PHEASANT DANGER

NO CONFIT FOR OLD MEN

AMERICAN HISTORY EGGS

POACH ADAMS

ABOUT A BOIL

FRIED EGG THE 13TH

CRACK TO THE FUTURE

YOLK BACK MOUNTAIN

FOR WHOM THE SHELL TOLLS

WILLIAM SHAKESPEARE'S OMELET

EGG WHITE & SEVEN DWARVES

LAID RUNNER

SERVES	25 SQUARES
PREPARATION TIME	10 MINUTES
COOKING TIME	1 HOUR

2¼ sticks (250g) butter, cubed, plus extra for greasing

9oz (250g) dark chocolate (minimum 65% cocoa solids), broken into pieces

1½ cups (300g) golden superfine (caster) sugar

4 eggs

1½ cups (180g) all-purpose (plain) flour

½ cup (50g) Dutch-processed cocoa powder, plus extra for dusting (optional)

¼ teaspoon baking powder

⅓ cup (75g) crystallized ginger, chopped

2½oz (70g) white chocolate chips

2½oz (70g) milk chocolate chips

GLACE VENTURA

Triple Chocolate and Ginger Brownies

Al-righty then. It's only fitting that a dish inspired by an animal protector be vegetarian. Chocolate is said to be an aphrodisiac—just make sure you don't make out with a man you thought was a woman.

- Preheat the oven to 325°F/160°C/Gas 3. Grease and line a 9-in (22-cm) square cake pan (tin) with baking paper and set aside.

- Melt the butter and dark chocolate in a bowl over a saucepan of simmering water. Stir occasionally until the chocolate is completely melted and smooth. Remove the chocolate from the heat and leave to cool for 5 minutes.

- Once the chocolate has cooled slightly, add the sugar and whisk in the eggs one at a time until well combined. Add the flour, cocoa powder, and baking powder, and use a wooden spoon to mix until just combined. Gently fold in the chopped ginger and chocolate chips.

- Pour the mixture into the prepared cake pan and bake for 45–50 minutes or until just set.

- Remove the brownies from the oven, dust with cocoa powder (optional), and slice into squares. Serve warm or at room temperature.

SERVES	4
PREPARATION TIME	15 MINUTES
COOKING TIME	1 HOUR

1 stick (125g) butter, cubed, plus extra for greasing

Heaping 1 cup (220g) superfine (caster) sugar

2 eggs

1¾ cups (225g) all-purpose (plain) flour

2 teaspoons ground cinnamon

1 teaspoon baking powder

½ cup (125ml) milk

1 apple, peeled, cored, and diced

⅓ cup (45g) dried cherries

⅓ cup (35g) chopped almonds, plus a few extra almonds to top loaf

LOAF ACTUALLY

Apple, Almond, and Dried Cherry Loaf

What better way to applaud this festive-themed romcom than with our spin on the old Christmas pudding? Like the movie, it's truly English and equal parts nutty, spicy, and sweet. Enjoy a slice with someone special and tell them, "Almond love with you."

- Preheat the oven to 325°F/170°C/Gas 3. Grease and line the base and sides of a 9 x 5-in. (23 x 13-cm) loaf pan (tin) with baking paper and set aside.

- In the bowl of an electric mixer, beat the butter and sugar on medium speed for 5 minutes or until pale and creamy. Add the eggs, one at a time, and beat well after each addition.

- In a separate bowl, sift together the flour, cinnamon, and baking powder.

- Add half of the flour mixture to the butter mixture, and continue to mix on a low speed until just combined. Add half the milk and mix through. Repeat with the remaining flour and milk until everything is combined. Do not over-mix, or the loaf will be tough.

- Add the apple, cherries, and almonds, and mix through using a spatula or wooden spoon until just combined. Transfer the mixture to the prepared pan and scatter over a few extra almonds. Bake for 1 hour—the loaf is ready when a skewer inserted into the middle of the loaf comes out clean.

- Serve the loaf warm or at room temperature.

CHAPTER 3 BEST HORROR AND CULT FLICKS

SERVES	4
PREPARATION TIME	15 MINUTES
COOKING TIME	25 MINUTES

1 tablespoon olive oil

1 tablespoon (15g) butter

1 onion, finely chopped

4 slices streaky bacon or pancetta, chopped

2 celery sticks, finely chopped

2 bay leaves

2 thyme sprigs

2¼lb (1kg) fresh clams

2 cups (500ml) chicken stock

12oz (350g) potatoes (such as Desiree, Yukon Gold, or similar), peeled and cut into 1¼in (3cm) pieces

⅓ cup (100ml) light (single) cream

½ cup (15g) chopped parsley leaves

Salt and freshly ground black pepper

Crackers or crusty bread, to serve

SILENCE OF THE CLAMS

Bacon and Clam Chowder

What meal would be perfect for Hannibal "The Cannibal" Lecter? Easy. Something with meat that can be fed through a mask. And this chowder is a whole lot nicer than a moth in the mouth. Enjoy it with a nice Chianti.

– Place a large saucepan over a medium heat. Once the pan is hot, add the olive oil, butter, onion, bacon, and celery. Fry for 8 minutes, or until soft and starting to brown. Add the bay leaves and thyme.

– Meanwhile, bring 2½ cups (600ml) of water to a simmer in another large saucepan. Add the clams, cover with a tight-fitting lid, and reduce the heat to low. Steam for 3–4 minutes or until the shells are open (discard any that are unopened). Drain the clams, reserving the liquid. Remove the meat from the shells and set aside.

– Add the stock and reserved clam liquid to the onion and bacon mixture. Bring to a simmer, add the potatoes, and cook for 10 minutes or until the potatoes are just tender. Add the clams, cream, and parsley, and cook for 5 minutes. Season with salt and pepper.

– Serve the chowder with crackers or crusty bread.

GNOCCHI HORROR SHOW

Ricotta Gnocchi with Bacon and Tomato Sauce

SERVES	4
PREPARATION TIME	10 MINUTES
COOKING TIME	40 MINUTES

1¼lb (600g) vine-ripened cherry tomatoes

2 tablespoons olive oil

1lb 2oz (500g) firm ricotta, from the deli

½ cup (50g) freshly grated Parmesan cheese, plus extra to serve

1 egg

1¼–1⅓ cups (150–200g) all-purpose (plain) flour

4 slices bacon, chopped

About 2 tablespoons (30g) butter

½ bunch basil leaves, picked

Salt and freshly ground black pepper

Sorry to mislead those of you looking for fishnets or Frank N. Furters. There is no seafood or sausage in this dish… or Meatloaf for that matter. But, like the movie, it is fairly cheesy.

- Preheat the oven to 400°F/200°C/Gas 6.

- Place the tomatoes on a large baking tray lined with baking paper. Drizzle with 1 tablespoon of the olive oil and roast in the oven for 20 minutes, or until the tomatoes begin to collapse. Remove from the oven and set aside.

- Put the ricotta, Parmesan cheese, egg, and flour in a bowl. Mix the ingredients together until they form a sticky dough that comes away from the sides of the bowl. If the mixture feels too wet, add some more flour. Divide the mixture into four, and roll each portion into thin lengths. Cut each length into ½-in (2-cm) sized pieces to form the gnocchi and place on a floured tray.

- Bring a large saucepan or cooking pot of salted water to a boil. Add a quarter of the gnocchi and cook for 2–3 minutes or until they rise to the surface. Transfer the cooked gnocchi to a plate lined with some paper towel. Repeat this process three times with the remaining batches of gnocchi.

- Heat the other tablespoon of olive oil in a large skillet (frying pan) over a medium heat. Add the bacon and fry until it begins to turn golden. Add half the roasted tomatoes and use the back of a fork to squash them to form a sauce. Add the butter and stir until melted. Season with salt and pepper. Add the cooked gnocchi to the sauce and stir gently to coat.

- Add the remaining tomatoes and serve with a scattering of basil and extra Parmesan cheese.

SERVES	8
PREPARATION TIME	10 MINUTES, PLUS REFRIGERATION OVERNIGHT
COOKING TIME	1½ HOURS

1 teaspoon olive oil

25 slices prosciutto

1lb 12oz (800g) ground (minced) chicken

3oz (80g) ground (minced) pork

3 garlic cloves, crushed

¼ cup (5g) chopped parsley leaves

½ cup (125ml) sherry

3 eggs, lightly beaten

½ cup (95g) chopped dried apricots

¼ cup (40g) shelled unsalted pistachio nuts

Salt and freshly ground black pepper

Toasted bread, to serve

TERRINE WOLF

Chicken, Pork, and Apricot Terrine

Given his name, Michael J. Fox was always the front-runner to play a wolf. Get your canines into this fancy French meatloaf—it'll put hairs on your chest. Howwwl.

- Preheat the oven to 350°F/180°C/Gas 4.

- Grease a 1lb (450g) loaf pan (tin) or terrine dish with the oil and line with the prosciutto slices. Overlap the slices slightly and ensure the edges are overhanging the pan or dish.

- Place the remaining ingredients in a large bowl and season generously with salt and pepper. Use your hands to mix the ingredients together thoroughly. Once combined, carefully pack the mixture into the lined pan or dish, press down to flatten, and cover with the overhanging prosciutto. Cover the top of the pan or dish with baking paper and then seal tightly with aluminum foil.

- Place the terrine in a large roasting pan. Pour in boiling water until it reaches halfway up the pan or dish. Carefully transfer to the oven and cook for 1½ hours. Once the terrine is cooked, remove from the pan, discard the foil and baking paper, and leave to cool completely.

- Once cool, drain any excess juices and cover again with foil. Cut a piece of thick cardstock (card) to fit the top of the pan or dish. Place on top of the terrine and weigh down with cans. Transfer to the refrigerator to chill overnight.

- To serve the terrine, remove from the refrigerator and leave to reach room temperature. Cut into thick slices and serve with toasted bread.

CLOSE ENCOUNTERS...

RETURN OF THE RIBEYE

THE LEGEND OF BEEF BURGUNDY

BILL & TED'S BOGUS JERKY

WHO FLAMED ROGER RABBIT?

THE LOIN RANGER

THE MERCHANT OF VENISON

21 RUMP STREET

BURGER ON THE ORIENT EXPRESS

THE WIZARD OF OX

THE PELICAN BEEF

THE DEVIL WEARS PARMA

MEAT THE FOCKERS

...OF THE FURRED KIND

TARTAR RECALL

THE GIRL WITH THE DRAGON RAGU

A FLEISCH CALLED WANDA

GRAN CHORIZO

CLIFF BANGER

WURST SIDE STORY

HOTDOG MILLIONAIRE

SERVES	12
PREPARATION TIME	10 MINUTES
COOKING TIME	12 MINUTES

THE FIG LEBOWSKI

Roasted Figs with Buffalo Mozzarella, Basil, and Prosciutto

These yummy treats are inspired by the Coen brothers' cult classic. So chuck on your bowling shoes, channel "The Dude" and strike up the oven.

12 figs

1 large ball of buffalo mozzarella (around 9oz/250g), torn into 12 pieces

12 basil leaves

6 thin slices prosciutto, halved lengthwise

Salt and freshly ground black pepper

– Preheat the oven to 350°F/180°C/Gas 4. Line a baking tray with baking paper.

– Cut a cross from top to bottom in each fig, being careful not to cut all the way through. Place a piece of mozzarella and a basil leaf inside each fig. Wrap each fig in a slice of prosciutto. Transfer the figs to the prepared tray and season with salt and pepper.

– Place the tray in the oven and cook for 12 minutes, or until the mozzarella has melted.

– Serve the roasted figs warm.

Tip: Perhaps enjoy with a White Russian cocktail?

SERVES	4
PREPARATION TIME	5 MINUTES
COOKING TIME	15 MINUTES

INGLORIOUS PASTAS

Pea, Bacon, and Ricotta Alfredo

5 cups (500g) dried fusilli

1 cup (150g) frozen peas

1 tablespoon olive oil

3 slices lean bacon, finely chopped

1lb 2oz (500g) ricotta

½ cup (125ml) water (reserved from the cooked pasta)

Zest of 1 lemon

2 tablespoons chopped chives

½ cup (50g) freshly grated Parmesan cheese, plus extra to serve

Salt and freshly ground black pepper

In this typically Tarantino, genre-blurring, violent classic, Brad Pitt and his fellow Nazi-hunting "basterds" pretend, unconvincingly, to be Italian. I consider my alfredo to be somewhat more authentic. And for Jewish diners, please feel free to replace the bacon with something kosher.

- Cook the pasta according to the packet instructions. Add the peas 1 minute before the pasta has finished cooking. Drain the pasta and peas, and set aside ½ cup (125ml) of the cooking water.

- While the pasta is cooking, heat the olive oil in a large skillet (frying pan) over a medium heat. Add the bacon and fry for 5–6 minutes or until crispy.

- Reduce the heat to low and add the ricotta and reserved pasta water to the pan. Stir until combined. Add the drained pasta and peas, lemon zest, chives, and Parmesan cheese. Season generously with salt and pepper, and then gently toss to coat the pasta with the ricotta sauce.

- Serve immediately, along with an extra sprinkling of Parmesan cheese.

SERVES	2
PREPARATION TIME	5 MINUTES
COOKING TIME	10 MINUTES

EDWARD CAESARHANDS

Chargrilled Asparagus with Caesar Dressing

Rumor has it Edward Scissorhand's pale complexion was attributed to his inadequate consumption of green vegetables. Hence, our interpretation of Tim Burton's masterpiece is of a young man with asparagus for fingers. This is his story.

¼ baguette, cut into cubes

3 tablespoons olive oil

1lb (450g) asparagus spears, stalks trimmed

Salt and freshly ground black pepper

For the Caesar Dressing:

¾ cup (175ml) mayonnaise

½ cup (50g) freshly grated Parmesan cheese, plus extra to serve

1 garlic clove, crushed

Zest of 1 lemon, plus 2 tablespoons lemon juice

1 teaspoon Dijon mustard

1 teaspoon Worcestershire sauce

- To make the dressing, place the mayonnaise, Parmesan cheese, garlic, lemon juice and zest, Dijon mustard, and Worcestershire sauce in a small bowl and mix well. Set aside.

- Toss the bread cubes in half the olive oil and season with salt. Place the bread under a broiler (grill) set to a low heat and broil (grill) for 3 minutes, or until the cubes are toasted and golden on each side. Remove the croutons from the broiler and set aside.

- Increase the broiler temperature to high. Place the asparagus in a large dish, toss with the remaining olive oil, and season with salt and pepper. Place the asparagus under the broiler for 4–5 minutes, or until cooked and charred. Transfer to a serving platter.

- Drizzle the asparagus with the dressing and top with the croutons and some extra Parmesan cheese. Eat with a fork, but be careful not to prick the waterbed.

SERVES	4
PREPARATION TIME	15 MINUTES
COOKING TIME	1 HOUR 10 MINUTES

I KNOW WHAT YOU DID LAST SUPPER

Not-So-Scary Cottage Pie

1 tablespoon olive oil

1 onion, chopped

2 carrots, chopped

1½lb (700g) ground (minced) beef

2 tablespoons chopped thyme leaves

½ cup (100ml) red wine

2 tablespoons tomato paste (purée)

1 tablespoon Worcestershire sauce

2 cups (500ml) beef stock

2lb 12oz (1.2kg) potatoes, peeled and cut into large chunks

6½ tablespoons (85g) butter, cubed

2 tablespoons whole milk

1 cup (100g) grated Cheddar cheese

Salt and freshly ground black pepper

This scrumptious and comforting pie is anything but a nightmare. Dish this up and all your guests will be terrorizing you for more.

– Preheat the oven to 350°F/180°C/Gas 4.

– Heat the olive oil in a medium saucepan over a medium heat. Add the onion and carrots, and cook for 4–5 minutes, or until softened. Add the beef and thyme, and cook for a further 8–10 minutes or until browned on all sides. Add the wine, tomato paste (purée), and Worcestershire sauce. Stir to combine. Pour in the stock and bring to a simmer. Reduce the heat to low and cover with a lid. Simmer for 35 minutes.

– While the beef is cooking, place the potatoes in a large saucepan and cover with water. Bring to a boil over a medium heat and simmer for 10 minutes, or until the potatoes are tender. Drain into a colander and return the potatoes to the pan. Add the butter, milk, and cheese. Season with salt and pepper, and then mash the potatoes.

– Transfer the beef to a deep ovenproof pie or casserole dish, and top with the mashed potato. Place the pie in the oven and bake for 20–25 minutes, or until the mash starts to turn golden.

– Remove the pie from the oven and leave to cool for 5 minutes before serving.

SERVES	4
PREPARATION TIME	15 MINUTES
COOKING TIME	12 MINUTES

DONNIE TACO

Grilled Fish Tacos with Avocado Salsa

2 avocados, peeled and cubed

½ red onion, finely chopped

1 red chili pepper, finely chopped

¼ cup (5g) chopped cilantro (coriander) leaves

2 tablespoons extra virgin olive oil

Zest and juice of 2 limes

1¼lb (550g) skinless white fish fillets (such as ling, halibut, brill, barramundi), cut into large chunks

8 soft tortillas

⅓ cup (80ml) mayonnaise

Salt and freshly ground black pepper

The mind-bending, psychological horror *Donnie Darko* inspires these equally hypnotic Mexican delights. Before a jet engine crashes into your bedroom in 28 days, be a good Doomsday prepper and load up on these ingredients.

– To make the salsa, place the avocado, onion, chili pepper, cilantro (coriander), 1 tablespoon of the olive oil, and the juice and zest of 1 lime in a medium bowl. Season with salt and pepper, then toss gently to combine the salsa. Set aside.

– Preheat a barbecue or grill pan to a high heat. Drizzle the fish all over with the juice and zest of the other lime and the remaining olive oil. Season with salt and pepper.

– Once the barbecue or grill pan is hot, cook the fish for 8 minutes, or until cooked through, turning once halfway through the cooking time. Place the fish on a board or plate and cover with aluminum foil to keep warm.

– Place the tortillas on the barbecue or grill, and cook for 1 minute on each side or until warm and slightly charred. Transfer the tortillas to a plate.

– Place the fish and salsa on the tortillas. Drizzle a small amount of mayonnaise on top, then wrap up the tortillas and serve immediately.

THE TEXAS CHAINSAW MOUSSAKA

Easy Moussaka

<table>
<tr><td>SERVES</td><td>4–6</td></tr>
<tr><td>PREPARATION TIME</td><td>25 MINUTES</td></tr>
<tr><td>COOKING TIME</td><td>1 HOUR</td></tr>
</table>

4 large potatoes, peeled and cut into ½in (1cm) slices

2 eggplants (aubergines), cut into ½in (1cm) slices

4 tablespoons olive oil

1 onion, chopped

1¼lb (600g) ground (minced) lamb

2 garlic cloves, chopped

1 teaspoon ground coriander

1 teaspoon dried cilantro (coriander)

1 teaspoon ground cumin

⅔ cup (150ml) red wine

14oz (400g) can chopped tomatoes

2 tablespoons tomato paste (purée)

3 eggs

1½ cups (350ml) Greek yogurt

1¾ cups (180g) grated Cheddar cheese

Salt and freshly ground black pepper

The Texas Chainsaw Massacre was so violent that it was banned across many countries. My moussaka is far less terrifying for any part-time cook. But with so many slices of eggplant (aubergine) and potatoes required, a chainsaw wouldn't go astray. But, then again, the sound of the two-stroke engine in the kitchen might seem like overkill.

– Cook the potato slices in a large saucepan of boiling salted water for 12 minutes or until just tender. Drain the potato slices, place on a large plate or tray, and leave to cool.

– Meanwhile, preheat a grill pan over a high heat. Drizzle half the olive oil over the eggplant (aubergine) and grill for 4 minutes on each side or until charred. Remove from the grill pan and set aside.

– Heat the remaining oil in a large, heavy-based, deep-sided skillet (frying pan) over a medium-high heat. Add the onion and sauté for 5 minutes or until soft. Add the lamb, garlic, herbs, and spices. Fry for 10 minutes or until the meat has completely browned. Add the wine, tomatoes, and tomato paste (purée), and season with salt and pepper. Stir to combine. Bring to a simmer and cook for 20 minutes.

– Meanwhile, preheat the oven to 375°F/190°C/Gas 5.

– Arrange some of the potato slices in an even layer on the base of a deep ovenproof dish. Add some of the eggplant to create a second layer, and then some of the lamb mixture to create a third layer. Repeat to create more layers of potatoes, eggplant, and the lamb mixture, and finish with a layer of eggplant.

– Mix the eggs, yogurt, and cheese together in medium bowl and season with salt and pepper. Pour the mixture over the eggplant and transfer the dish to the oven. Bake for 35 minutes or until golden. Remove from the oven and leave to rest for 5 minutes before serving.

2 tablespoons olive oil

2 garlic cloves, crushed

3 teaspoons ground sumac

Zest and juice of 1 lemon

3½lb (1.6kg) roasting (whole) chicken, boned and butterflied (ask your butcher to do this)

Salt and freshly ground black pepper

For the Green Harissa:

1 teaspoon cumin seeds

1 teaspoon coriander seeds

¼ cup (50ml) extra virgin olive oil

3 long green chili peppers

2 cups (60g) baby spinach

1 cup (25g) chopped cilantro (coriander) leaves

1 garlic clove, crushed

1 tablespoon water

NATURAL BORN GRILLERS

Butterflied Chicken with Green Harissa

The original screenplay for *Natural Born Killers* was written by Quentin Tarantino. Adjusted and produced, it went on to become one of the most controversial films ever released due to its graphic content and the copycat crimes it inspired. Warning: our dish also runs the risk of spawning delicious copycats.

– Place the olive oil, garlic, sumac, and lemon juice and zest in a large, deep-sided roasting pan or large baking dish. Season with salt and pepper, then mix to combine. Add the chicken and rub with the mixture. Cover with plastic wrap (clingfilm), refrigerate, and leave to marinate for 30 minutes.

– Preheat the oven to 425°F/220°C/Gas 7. Remove the chicken from the refrigerator and leave to stand for 10 minutes or until it reaches room temperature. Remove the plastic wrap. Transfer to the oven and cook for 40 minutes or until the skin is browned and the chicken is cooked through.

– To make the green harissa, toast the cumin and coriander seeds in a small skillet (frying pan) over a medium heat for 2 minutes or until aromatic. Transfer to a mortar and pestle (or a spice grinder) and grind to a powder. Add to a food processor, along with the remaining harissa ingredients. Blend until smooth.

– Once the chicken is cooked, drizzle over some of the harissa and serve. Any remaining harissa can be kept for up to 3 days in the refrigerator.

THE GREATEST LOINS...

"YOU HAD ME AT HALAL."

"NOBODY PUTS BABY
IN THE KORMA."

"THE HILLS ARE ALIVE WITH
THE SOUND OF MUESLI."

"HE'S NOT THE MASALA.
HE'S A VERY NAUGHTY BOY."

"SINGING IN LORRAINE, JUST SINGING IN LORRAINE"

★ ★ ★ ★ ★

...OF ALL TIME

"YIPEE KI-YAY
MOTHER DUKKAH!"

"LUKE. I AM
YOUR FAVA."

"I FEEL THE NEED,
THE NEED FOR SWEDE."

"OH I'M SORRY, DID I BREAK
YOUR DEGUSTATION?"

"I SEE DEAD PICKLE."

★ ★ ★ ★ ★

SERVES	12 BARS
PREPARATION TIME	10 MINUTES
COOKING TIME	20 MINUTES, PLUS 2 HOURS' CHILLING TIME

SNACK TO THE FUTURE

Old-School Granola Bars

Wouldn't it be neat if you could travel back in time with your hoverboard, self-lacing Nike high-tops, and DeLorean? Back to a time when synthetic flavors, colors, and preservatives weren't yet conceived. Well, these natural wholesome goodies are just what "The Doc" ordered.

2½ cups (250g) traditional porridge (rolled) oats

½ cup (55g) chopped almonds

5 tablespoons (60g) butter, cubed, plus extra for greasing

⅓ cup (115g) honey

¼ cup (50g) light brown sugar

½ teaspoon vanilla extract

Pinch of salt

½ cup (90g) chopped dried fruit (such as apricots, cranberries, and raisins)

½ cup (90g) milk chocolate chips

– Preheat the oven to 350°F/180°C/Gas 4. Grease and line the base and sides of an 8-in (20-cm) square baking pan (tin) with baking paper.

– Spread the oats and almonds evenly on another large baking tray. Transfer to the oven to toast for 10–12 minutes, carefully stirring halfway through the cooking time. Once the oats and almonds are lightly toasted, transfer to a large bowl.

– Meanwhile, heat the butter, honey, sugar, vanilla extract, and salt in a small saucepan over a medium heat. Stir regularly for approximately 5 minutes. Once the sugar has dissolved and the butter has melted, add the mixture to the oats and mix thoroughly to combine. Leave to cool for 5 minutes before stirring through the dried fruit and half the chocolate chips.

– Transfer the mixture to the prepared pan and use the back of a spoon or your fingers to press it down firmly and evenly. Scatter over the remaining chocolate chips and press them firmly onto the top of the mixture.

– Cover the pan with plastic wrap (clingfilm) and refrigerate for 2 hours. Once chilled, remove from the refrigerator and cut into 12 bars.

– Store in an airtight container, either in the refrigerator or at room temperature for up to a week.

BEST ACTRESS OF ALL TIME

And the nominees are...

ANGELINA JELLY	ECLAIR DANES
ATE HUDSON	EGG RYAN
BRAN HATHAWAY	ELIZABETH JUS
CAKE WINSLET	ELLEN SAGE
CATE BLANCH IT	GLACE KELLY
CELERY SWANK	GLENN CLOVES
CHERRIES THERON	GOLDIE PRAWN
CHEW BARRYMORE	GWYNETH POULTRY
CREMA WATSON	HARISSA TOMEI
CURRY MULLIGAN	HELEN MIRIN
DIANE EATEN	HONEY BERRY

INGRID BURGERMAN	MARLIN MONROE
ISABELLA BROCCOLINI	MARROW STREEP
JANE FONDANT	NAOMI WOKS
JENNIFER ANISEED	PATRICIA COURGETTE
JENNIFER CANNOLI	PENNE ZELLWEGER
JENNIFER GARNISH	SALSA HAYEK
JULIA RABBITS	SANDRA POLLOCK
JULIENNED MOORE	SCALLOP JOHANSSON
JUNIPER LAWRENCE	TILDA SWEETEN
KATHERINE BAGEL	WHOPPER GOLDBERG
KRISTEN SUET	WINONA CIDER
LINSEED LOHAN	ZOOEY BÉCHAMEL

SERVES	6
PREPARATION TIME	20 MINUTES, PLUS 24 HOURS' COOLING AND REFRIGERATION TIME
COOKING TIME	20 MINUTES

PLANET OF THE GRAPES

Vanilla Panna Cotta with Marinated Grapes

2 cups (500ml) heavy (double) cream

¾ cup (200ml) whole milk

Scant 1 cup (180g) superfine (caster) sugar

1 vanilla bean (pod), split open and the seeds removed

3 leaves gold leaf gelatin

For the Marinated Grapes:

2 cups (200g) red seedless grapes, washed and stems removed

1 cup (250ml) white wine

1 tablespoon balsamic vinegar

1 tablespoon sugar

2 teaspoons finely grated orange zest

Primitive humans? Talking apes? It's all upside down. A bit like the upturned "cooked cream" pudding we know as panna cotta. This one sounds tough to make, but really it's for chimps.

– To make the marinated grapes, place the grapes in a large, nonreactive bowl. Place the wine, vinegar, sugar, and lemon zest in a small pan over a medium heat. Once the mixture reaches a boil, remove from the heat immediately. Pour the mixture over the grapes and leave the mixture to return to room temperature. Cover the bowl with plastic wrap (clingfilm) and transfer to the refrigerator for 24 hours (or up to a week).

– Place the cream, milk, sugar, and scraped vanilla seeds and bean (pod) in a large pan. Stir over a low-medium heat and slowly bring to a boil. When the mixture just reaches a boil, remove from the heat immediately.

– While the cream mixture is heating through, place the gelatin leaves in a shallow dish and cover with cold water to soften for 5 minutes. Remove the gelatin and squeeze out any excess water. Whisk the gelatin into the cream mixture until dissolved.

– Allow the mixture to cool slightly and then strain through a sieve into a pitcher (jug). Pour into six 4-fl-oz (120-ml) capacity pudding molds, and transfer to the refrigerator for 5 hours or until set. The panna cottas should still have a slight wobble once set.

– Remove the panna cottas from the refrigerator and run a sharp knife around the edge of the molds. Dip the molds briefly into hot water and then use your fingers to gently loosen the panna cottas from the edges. Turn upside down to release the panna cottas from the molds.

– Serve each panna cotta with a spoonful of cold marinated grapes.

1⅔ cups (200g) all-purpose (plain) flour, sifted

4 eggs

2½ cups (600ml) milk

1⅔ cups (400ml) buttermilk

About 5 tablespoons (60g) butter

14oz (400g) firm ricotta

1 tablespoon honey

For the Citrus Compote:

3 tablespoons superfine (caster) sugar

2 blood oranges, peeled and segmented, with pips and pith removed (reserve the juice)

1 lemon, peeled and segmented, with pips and pith removed (reserve the juice and zest)

CREPE FEAR

Ricotta Crepes with Citrus Compote

If you're fresh out of the clink and out for vengeance, like *Cape Fear*'s lead character Max Cady, why not slit a few blood oranges and beat some eggs while you plot your next move.

– To make the compote, heat the sugar and citrus segments and juices in a large (skillet) frying pan over a medium heat. Stir gently and cook for 2–3 minutes, or until the sugar has dissolved and the fruit begins to soften. Set aside to cool.

– Place the flour in a large bowl and make a well in the center. In a separate bowl, whisk together the eggs, milk, and buttermilk until combined. Slowly pour the mixture into the flour well while continuing to whisk. Continue to whisk for 1–2 minutes, or until the mixture is smooth and there are no lumps.

– Heat a small amount of the butter in a crepe pan or nonstick skillet (frying pan) over a medium-high heat. Once the butter has melted, pour a small ladle of crepe batter into the pan and swirl around until there is a thin, even layer covering the base. Cook for 1–2 minutes until the crepe is slightly browned, then turn over and cook on the other side for a further minute. Turn the crepe out onto a plate and repeat for the remainder of the batter.

– In a medium bowl, mix together the ricotta, honey, and lemon zest. Set aside.

– To serve, spread a spoonful of the ricotta mixture evenly over each crepe. Fold the crepes in half and then in half again. Place the filled crepes on a plate and top with the citrus compote.

PRISCILLA, QUEEN OF THE DESSERT

FUDGE DREDD
ADMIT ONE · ADMIT ONE

THE GOOD SHERBERT
ADMIT ONE · ADMIT ONE

GLAZE OF THUNDER
ADMIT ONE · ADMIT ONE

CANNOLI UGLY
ADMIT ONE · ADMIT ONE

COCOA BEFORE CHANEL

SPONGECAKE SQUAREPANTS
ADMIT ONE · ADMIT ONE

ANY GIVEN SUNDAE
ADMIT ONE · ADMIT ONE

MY BEST FRIEND'S WEDDING
ADMIT ONE · ADMIT ONE

VICKI CROSTINI BARCELONA
ADMIT ONE · ADMIT ONE

CRUMBLE IN THE JUNGLE
ADMIT ONE · ADMIT ONE

MOUSSE CONGENIALITY
ADMIT ONE · ADMIT ONE

ÉCLAIR WITCH PROJECT

AMERICAN FRUITY

ADMIT ONE ROBIN HOOD QUINCE OF THIEVES ADMIT ONE

ADMIT ONE MEDJOOL OF THE NILE ADMIT ONE

ADMIT ONE MANGO UNCHAINED ADMIT ONE

ADMIT ONE RAISIN ARIZONA ADMIT ONE

PEACH PERFECT

ADMIT ONE MELON ROUGE ADMIT ONE

HARRY POTTER AND THE CHAMBER OF CITRUS

ADMIT ONE A BEAUTIFUL RIND ADMIT ONE

ADMIT ONE THE PRINCE AND THE PAW PAW ADMIT ONE

CHAPTER 4 BEST ACTION MOVIES

14oz (400g) raw shrimp (prawns), peeled and deveined

Juice of 3 lemons

Juice of 3 limes and zest of 1 lime

1 red chili pepper, finely chopped

1 shallot, finely chopped

½ avocado, peeled and finely chopped

2 tablespoons finely chopped cilantro (coriander) leaves

Pinch of sugar

2 teaspoons olive oil

Salt and freshly ground black pepper

THE PRAWN IDENTITY

Prawn and Citrus Ceviche

Drawing inspiration from the first flick in the Bourne Series, this is the tale of Jason Prawn, a tangy crustacean with multiple identities. He might have amnesia, but you won't forget this starter.

- Bring a saucepan of water to a boil and blanch the shrimp (prawns) for 30 seconds. Drain and chill immediately in a bowl of iced water. Pat dry with some paper towel and cut into small ¾in (2cm) pieces.

- Place the shrimp in a glass or ceramic bowl and cover with the lemon juice, lime juice, and lime zest. Cover and refrigerate for 45 minutes.

- Drain the juice from the shrimp. Add the chili pepper, shallot, avocado, cilantro (coriander), sugar, and olive oil to the bowl. Season with salt and pepper, and mix well.

- Serve the prawns immediately in small glasses or bowls.

THE FISH ELEMENT

AMERICAN SNAPPER

REVOLUTIONARY ROE

THE LIFE OF BRINE

SEABASS IN SEATTLE

THERE'S SOMETHING ABOUT MORAY

THE CODFATHER

FIFTY SHADES OF CRAY

BUTCH CASSIDY & THE SARDINES KID

BEYOND REASONABLE TROUT

HERRING BROCKOVICH

AMERICAN MUSSEL

MR HOLLAND'S OCTOPUS

GORILLAS IN THE BISQUE

KARATE SQUID

HAIL, SEASON!

THE HERB LOCKER

THE DA VINCI CLOVE

21 GARAMS

MARJORAM CALL

THE THYME TRAVELER'S WIFE

ANISE IN WONDERLAND

ICE SAGE

MULHOLLAND CHIVE

NOTTING DILL

CITIZEN CAYENNE

2001: A SPICE ODYSSEY

SAFFRON YEARS IN TIBET

SERVES	6
PREPARATION TIME	15 MINUTES
COOKING TIME	40 MINUTES

BRAVE TART

Zucchini, Feta, and Speck Tart

Braveheart was all about revolting… revolting against the English monarchy. On the other hand, our tribute tart is anything but yuck. If you're a bit blue in the face, enjoy it warm.

1½ tablespoons (20g) butter, plus extra for greasing

1 onion, finely chopped

5½oz (150g) speck, chopped into small pieces

3 large zucchini (courgettes), grated

1½ cups (150g) grated Cheddar cheese

½ cup (70g) crumbled feta

1¼ cups (150g) self-rising flour

6 eggs, lightly beaten

⅓ cup (100ml) vegetable oil

⅓ cup (10g) chopped herbs (such as parsley, thyme, and tarragon)

Salt and freshly ground black pepper

– Preheat the oven to 350°F/180°C/Gas 4. Grease and line a large, non-stick tray-bake pan (tin), measuring 12 x 8 x 1¼ in/ 30 x 20 x 3cm, with baking paper.

– Melt the butter in a medium skillet (frying pan) over a medium-heat. Once melted, add the onion and speck, and stir gently for 5 minutes or until the onion softens and the speck begins to brown. Remove from the heat and set aside to cool slightly.

– Using a colander, squeeze the grated zucchini (courgettes) thoroughly to remove any excess liquid. Place the zucchini in a large bowl with the Cheddar cheese, feta, flour, eggs, oil, herbs, and the cooled onion and speck mixture. Season with salt and pepper, and stir well to combine all the ingredients.

– Pour the mixture into the prepared tray-bake pan, transfer to the oven, and cook for 30 minutes or until puffed and golden. Remove the tart from the oven and serve warm or at room temperature.

SERVES	4
PREPARATION TIME	15 MINUTES
COOKING TIME	1 HOUR

SLAW OF THE WORLDS

Baked Sweet Potato with Kale Slaw

4 small sweet potatoes (each about 9oz/250g)

4½oz (130g) kale, shredded and stems removed

7oz (200g) red cabbage, shredded and core removed

2 carrots, shredded or grated

3 scallions (spring onions), finely sliced

¼ cup (5g) chopped cilantro (coriander) leaves

4 tablespoons extra virgin olive oil

For the dressing:

½ cup (125g) natural yogurt

1 garlic clove, crushed

1 teaspoon Dijon mustard

3 tablespoons olive oil

Juice of ½ lemon

Salt and freshly ground black pepper

Steven Spielberg's epic disaster thriller *War of the Worlds* was an adaptation of H.G. Wells' novel of the same name. My own adaptation makes a few notable additions, swapping pure evil for pure goodness, carnage for cabbage, and extraterrestrials for extra vegetables.

- Preheat the oven to 400°F/200°C/Gas 6.

- Place the potatoes on a baking tray lined with baking paper and cook for 1 hour, or until tender when pierced with a knife.

- To make the dressing, whisk all the ingredients together in a small bowl and season with salt and pepper.

- Place the kale, cabbage, carrots, scallions (spring onions), cilantro (coriander), and dressing in a large bowl, and toss together.

- Once the potatoes are cooked, remove from the oven, cut a slit in each lengthwise, and open slightly. Season each potato with salt and pepper, and drizzle over the extra virgin olive oil.

- Divide the slaw evenly between the sweet potatoes. Serve immediately.

SERVES	4–6
PREPARATION TIME	15 MINUTES
COOKING TIME	45 MINUTES

POINT BAKE

Ricotta Cannelloni with Tomato and Spinach Sauce

We believe that when Johnny Utah (Keanu Reeves) famously muttered, "I caught my first tube this morning, Sir" he actually had cannelloni on his mind. So grommets, it's time to swap your sunscreen for olive oil, your fins for tins, and your wax for mozzarella.

2 tablespoons olive oil

2 x 14oz (400g) cans chopped tomatoes

4 garlic cloves, crushed

Small handful basil leaves

3⅓ cups (100g) baby spinach

2 cups (500g) ricotta

Zest of 1 lemon

2½ cups (250g) grated mozzarella

7oz (200g) dried cannelloni

Salt and freshly ground black pepper

- Preheat the oven to 400°F/200°C/Gas 6.

- Heat the olive oil in a medium saucepan over a medium heat. Add the tomatoes and three of the garlic cloves, and bring to a boil. Reduce the heat, and simmer for 10 minutes or until the sauce thickens. Add the basil and spinach, and season with salt and pepper. Stir through until the basil and spinach have wilted.

- Place the ricotta, lemon zest, remaining garlic clove, and half the mozzarella in a bowl. Season with salt and pepper, then mix well to combine. Fill the cannelloni tubes with the cheese mixture, using a piping bag or small spoon, and set aside.

- Spoon half the tomato and basil sauce into an ovenproof dish, then place the filled cannelloni tubes side by side in the dish. Top with the remainder of the tomato sauce, then sprinkle over the remaining mozzarella.

- Transfer to the oven and bake for 30–35 minutes, or until the cheese is golden and the cannelloni is cooked through. Serve immediately.

Tip: As a tribute to the *Point Break* cameo appearance of Anthony Kiedis, add a finely chopped Red Hot Chili Pepper for extra zing.

SERVES	6–8
PREPARATION TIME	5 MINUTES
COOKING TIME	25 MINUTES

1 sourdough, Vienna, or Pane di Casa loaf

7 tablespoons (100g) softened butter

2 garlic cloves, crushed

1 tablespoon chopped parsley leaves

1 red chili pepper, finely chopped

2 cups (200g) grated mozzarella cheese

Salt and freshly ground black pepper

THE HUNT FOR BREAD OCTOBER

Quick Garlic and Chili Bread

It's no surprise that this thriller, the plot of which revolves around a sub, inspired a dish about a breadstick... Soviet sourdough, that is. Bread is often a symbol of peace—a warm loaf would have been handy during the Cold War.

- Preheat the oven to 350°F/180°C/Gas 4.

- Make a diamond pattern in the loaf by using a bread knife to cut diagonal slices in both directions of the loaf, 2in (5cm) apart, without cutting all the way through the bread.

- In a small bowl, mix together the butter, garlic, parsley, and chili pepper. Season with salt and pepper.

- Spoon the butter mixture into the cuts in the bread, then spread out with a knife or the back of the spoon. Sprinkle the cheese into the cuts.

- Place the loaf on a baking tray and cover loosely with aluminum foil. Transfer to the oven and bake for 15 minutes, or until the cheese has just melted. Remove the foil from the tray and bake for a further 8 minutes, or until the cheese turns golden.

SERVES	2
PREPARATION TIME	10 MINUTES
COOKING TIME	40 MINUTES

JURASSIC PORK

Nutmeg-spiced Pork Loin with Red Wine Braised Cabbage

1lb 2oz–1lb 4oz
(500–600g) pork loin

1½ tablespoons olive oil

1 teaspoon ground
nutmeg

For the Braised Cabbage:

1½ tablespoons (20g)
butter

½ red onion, finely
chopped

½ red cabbage, sliced

½ red apple, peeled,
cored, and finely
chopped

½ cup (125ml) red wine

12 tablespoons
cranberry sauce

Salt and freshly ground
black pepper

Get your fossils around this terrifyingly delicious dish... a main course 65 million years in the making. It'll bring you back from extinction.

- To make the braised cabbage, place a large saucepan over a medium heat and add the butter. Once the butter has melted, add the onion and sauté for 3–4 minutes or until it begins to soften. Add the cabbage and apple, and cook for 5 minutes before adding the wine.

- Bring to a simmer and cook for a further 5 minutes. Reduce the heat to low, cover the pan with a lid, and cook for a further 15 minutes, stirring occasionally. Add the cranberry sauce, season with salt and pepper, and cover to keep warm until ready to serve.

- Rub the pork with the olive oil and nutmeg, then season with salt and pepper. Place the pork in a skillet (frying pan) or grill pan over a medium heat. Cook for 10–14 minutes until cooked through, turning frequently to brown on all sides. Transfer the pork to a warm plate and leave to rest for 5 minutes until cooked.

- Cut the pork into thick slices and serve with the braised cabbage.

SERVES	10
PREPARATION TIME	30 MINUTES
COOKING TIME	1½ HOURS

THE INCREDIBLE HOCK

Glazed Ham

This ham is one to marvel. It'll make any pro chef green with envy. Just don't overcook it or your guests might throw some cars and pop some buttons.

3½oz (100g) quince paste

¼ cup (50ml) white wine

3 tablespoons orange juice

1 tablespoon sherry vinegar

2 teaspoons mixed spice or pumpkin pie spice

2 tablespoons chopped rosemary leaves

⅔ cup (140g) brown sugar

1 leg of ham (around 11–13lb/5–6kg)

– Preheat the oven to 350°F/180°C/Gas 4.

– To make the glaze, heat the quince paste, wine, orange juice, sherry vinegar, mixed or pumpkin pie spice, and rosemary in a small saucepan over a medium heat. Stir until smooth. Add the brown sugar and continue to cook until the sugar has dissolved. Once the glaze becomes smooth and syrupy, remove the saucepan from the heat and set aside.

– Use a sharp knife to score around the shank of the ham leg, before peeling back and removing the skin. Score the fat in a diamond pattern, with each diamond about 1½–2in (4–5cm) wide and cutting ¼in (5mm) deep. Transfer the ham to a large roasting pan, add 1 cup (250ml) of water, and brush with half the glaze.

– Place in the preheated oven and roast for 1½ hours, brushing occasionally with the remaining glaze. Remove from the oven and rest for 10 minutes before serving.

INDIAN JONES AND THE RAITAS OF THE LOST ARK

Chicken Curry with Coconut and Cucumber Raita

2 tablespoons vegetable oil

4 fresh curry leaves

1 white onion, thinly sliced

2 garlic cloves, finely chopped

1 tablespoon tikka marsala paste

¾ cup (200ml) chicken stock

2 tablespoons tomato paste (purée)

14oz (400g) can chopped tomatoes

14oz (400g) can coconut milk

1lb 2oz (500g) boneless chicken thighs, chopped into 1¼in (3cm) pieces

Naan bread or steamed rice, to serve

For the raita:

1 large cucumber, peeled, deseeded, and chopped

1 cup (250g) natural yogurt

1 tablespoon shredded (desiccated) coconut

1 tablespoon finely chopped cilantro (coriander) leaves

1 teaspoon lime juice

Salt and freshly ground black pepper

SERVES	4
PREPARATION TIME	15 MINUTES
COOKING TIME	30 MINUTES

Raiders of the Lost Ark follows the race to unearth the "Ark of the Covenant" that is said to contain the tablets of the Ten Commandments. Our search discovers one of the Ten Condiments: raita (insert whip crack).

– To make the raita, place the cucumber, yogurt, coconut, cilantro (coriander), and lime juice in a small bowl. Season with salt and pepper, then stir all the ingredients together to combine. Set aside.

– To make the curry, heat 1 tablespoon of the oil in a large saucepan over a medium heat. Once the oil is hot, add the curry leaves and cook for 1 minute, or until aromatic. Add the onion and garlic, and sauté for 5 minutes or until softened and starting to caramelize. Stir in the marsala paste and continue cooking for 2 minutes, stirring regularly. Add the stock, tomato purée (paste), tomatoes, and coconut milk. Reduce the heat to low and simmer for 12 minutes while you cook the chicken.

– Heat the remaining oil in a large skillet (frying pan) over a medium-high heat. Add the chicken and cook for 8 minutes, or until golden and charred on all sides. Add the chicken to the curry and continue to cook for 5–8 minutes, or until the chicken is cooked through. Season with salt and pepper.

– Top the curry with a spoonful of the raita, then serve along with some naan bread or steamed rice.

SERVES	6–8
PREPARATION TIME	15 MINUTES
COOKING TIME	2 HOURS

2 tablespoons olive oil

2 onions, diced

2lb (900g) boneless leg of lamb, diced into 1¼in (3cm) pieces

2½ teaspoons ground cumin

1½ teaspoons ground cinnamon

1½ teaspoons ground turmeric

2½ tablespoons honey

1⅓ cups (250g) dried apricots

Salt and freshly ground black pepper

For the Jeweled Couscous:

3 tablespoons extra virgin olive oil

2⅔ cups (450g) couscous

1 cup (100g) chopped pistachio nuts

1 cup (150g) pomegranate seeds

½ cup (15g) chopped parsley leaves

¼ cup (5g) chopped mint leaves

Juice of 1 lemon

LAMBO: FIRST BLOOD

Lamb Tagine with Jeweled Couscous

This dish is inspired by ex-green beret John Rambo, a man with pistachio nuts the size of grenades. Rambo must lean on his survival training when he's driven into nearby mountains by crooked law enforcers. He also has to rely on outdoor campfire cooking. And what could be better than the trusty tagine?

– Preheat a large tagine or deep-sided, heavy-based saucepan over a medium heat.

– Once hot, add the olive oil and sauté the onions for 5 minutes, or until they begin to brown. Add the lamb and cook for 8–10 minutes, stirring until all the meat has browned. Add all the spices, season with salt and pepper, then stir well to coat the meat. Add the honey, then pour in enough boiling water to cover the ingredients. Reduce the heat to low and simmer for 1 hour, stirring regularly. Add the apricots and cook for a further 45 minutes, or until the lamb is very tender.

– While the lamb is cooking, mix half the extra virgin olive oil with the couscous in a large bowl until all the grains are coated. Pour over 2 cups (500ml) of boiling water, cover the bowl, and set aside for 15 minutes, or until all the water is absorbed and the couscous is tender. When ready, use a fork to fluff up the grains. Add the remaining ingredients, season with salt and pepper, and stir well to combine.

– Once the lamb is ready, season to taste and serve with the couscous.

PEEL HARBOR

Orange Drizzle Cake

2 sticks (225g) butter, softened, plus extra for greasing

Heaping 1½ cups (325g) superfine (caster) sugar

4 eggs

Finely grated zest and juice of 1 orange

1¾ cups (225g) self-rising flour

2 teaspoons baking powder

4 tablespoons milk

While *Pearl Harbor* was considered a bit of a lemon by film critics, my tribute cake is all orange. Before hunger attacks, raid the refrigerator and show off your baking skills with military precision.

- Preheat the oven to 325°F/160°C/Gas 3. Grease and line the base and sides of a large, non-stick tray-bake pan (tin), measuring 12 x 9 x 1½in/30 x 23 x 4cm, with baking paper.

- Mix the butter and 1 cup (225g) of the sugar in the bowl of an electric mixer on high speed for 3–4 minutes. Add the eggs, one at a time, and beat for 30 seconds between each addition. Add the orange zest, flour, baking powder, and milk, then beat on medium speed until just combined. Be careful not to over-mix. Transfer the mixture to the tray-bake pan, then use a spatula to level it out.

- Bake in the oven for 35 minutes—the cake is ready when a skewer inserted into the middle comes out clean. Once ready, remove the cake from the oven and leave to sit for 4–5 minutes to cool slightly.

- Meanwhile, place the orange juice and remaining ½ cup (100g) of sugar in a medium bowl, and whisk together.

- Carefully remove the cake from the pan before transferring to a board or serving plate. Pour over the juice, allowing the warm cake to absorb the juice and cool further before cutting it into squares and serving.

TEENAGE MUTANT GINGER TURTLES

Chewy Caramel and Ginger Bites

4½ cups (450g) pecan nut halves, toasted

¾ cup (175ml) light corn (golden) syrup

Heaping ½ cup (115g) superfine (caster) sugar

½ cup (100g) soft brown sugar

4 tablespoons (50g) butter, softened

1 teaspoon vanilla extract

2oz (55g) milk chocolate

¼ cup (55g) crystallized ginger, finely chopped

Few know that the Ninja Turtles were not only trained in ninjutsu by their sensei Splinter; they were also schooled in pâtisserie. These delicious little weapons don't really come from the sewers, but they are "the sh*t." Perfect after pizza.

– Line two large baking trays with baking paper. Arrange four or five pecan halves into small clusters on the trays and set aside.

– Add the syrup and sugars to a small saucepan. Mix well and place over a medium-high heat. Boil for 10 minutes or until the mixture reaches a temperature of 245°F (118°C) when carefully tested with a sugar thermometer. Remove from the heat and stir in the butter and vanilla extract until combined. Use a tablespoon to spoon the caramel over the pecan clusters. Leave to cool and set for 1 hour.

– Once the caramel is set, melt the chocolate in a small bowl placed over a saucepan half-filled with simmering water. Warm the chocolate over a low heat for 5 minutes or until smooth. Spoon the melted chocolate over the caramel, then sprinkle the bites with the chopped ginger. Chill for 20 minutes, before serving at room temperature.

SERVES	2
PREPARATION TIME	10 MINUTES, PLUS REFRIGERATION TIME

CHIA AND PRESENT DANGER

Coconut Chia Puddings with Mango and Raspberries

½ cup (80g) chia seeds

¾ cup (175ml) whole milk (or almond milk)

1 cup (250ml) coconut milk

1 tablespoon honey

½ teaspoon vanilla bean powder

Pinch of salt

To serve:

1 mango, peeled, deseeded, and diced

½ cup (65g) raspberries

½ tablespoon shredded (desiccated) coconut

These tropical flavor-bangs are inspired by the all-absorbing third installment in the *Agent Jack Ryan* series by Tom Clancy. I tell you what else is absorbing: chia. Chia seeds can absorb up to 12 times their weight in liquid.

– Place the chia seeds, milk, coconut milk, honey, vanilla bean powder, and salt in a medium bowl and stir until well combined. Place the chia mixture into a bowl or container and store in the refrigerator for 6 hours or overnight.

– When ready to serve, remove the chia pudding from the refrigerator. Layer the diced mango and raspberries into bowls or glasses, then top with the chia pudding.

– Finish the puddings with some pieces of mango and a few raspberries, then sprinkle with the coconut.

PASTA LA VISTA BABY!

INDEX

AND THAT'S A WRAP!